YEEZY

KENNY ABDO

Fly!
An Imprint of Abdo Zoom
abdobooks.com

abdobooks.com

Published by Abdo Zoom, a division of ABDO, P.O. Box 398166, Minneapolis, Minnesota 55339. Copyright © 2023 by Abdo Consulting Group, Inc. International copyrights reserved in all countries. No part of this book may be reproduced in any form without written permission from the publisher. Fly!™ is a trademark and logo of Abdo Zoom.

Printed in the United States of America, North Mankato, Minnesota.
052022
092022

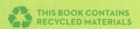

Photo Credits: Alamy, Getty Images, Shutterstock, Unsplash
Production Contributors: Kenny Abdo, Jennie Forsberg, Grace Hansen
Design Contributors: Candice Keimig, Neil Klinepier, Laura Graphenteen

Library of Congress Control Number: 2021950287

Publisher's Cataloging-in-Publication Data

Names: Abdo, Kenny, author.
Title: Yeezy / by Kenny Abdo.
Description: Minneapolis, Minnesota : Abdo Zoom, 2023 | Series: Hype brands | Includes online resources and index.
Identifiers: ISBN 9781098228583 (lib. bdg.) | ISBN 9781644948019 (pbk.) | ISBN 9781098229429 (ebook) | ISBN 9781098229849 (Read-to-Me ebook)
Subjects: LCSH: Clothing and dress--Juvenile literature. | Brand name products--Juvenile literature. | Fashion--Social aspects--Juvenile literature. | West, Kanye--Juvenile literature. | Popular culture--Juvenile literature. | Street life--Juvenile literature.
Classification: DDC 338.7--dc23

TABLE OF CONTENTS

Yeezy 4

Hype 8

All The Rage 14

Glossary 22

Online Resources 23

Index 24

YEEZY

Kanye West is one of the biggest names in entertainment. With hundreds of awards, seven **platinum records**, and sold-out concerts, the fashion runway was his next road to conquer.

Yeezy was a nickname given to West by rapper Jay-Z. Now Yeezy is considered one of the most influential sneaker and fashion brands in the world.

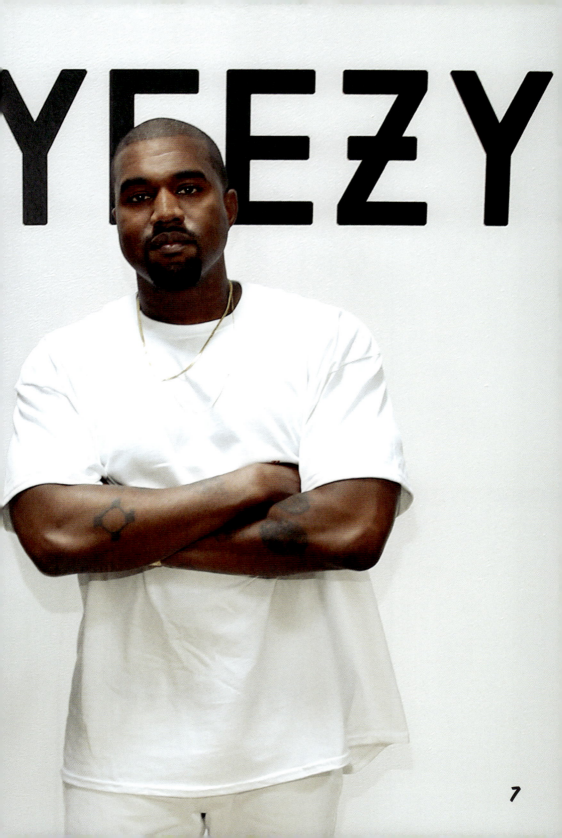

HYPE

Kanye Omari West was born on June 8, 1977, in Atlanta, Georgia. Raised in Chicago, young West often got in trouble with his teachers for sketching sneakers in class.

After years of success as a rapper, West wanted to take on another industry. He developed the Air Yeezy sneakers with Nike.

West wore the **prototype** for his 2008 Grammys performance.

In 2009, he started an **internship** at Fendi with Off-White's Virgil Abloh. The experience at Fendi pushed West to take his ambitions further. In 2011, West **debuted** his Dw collection at Paris Fashion Week.

ALL THE RAGE

In 2015, West revealed his Yeezy clothing line. Season 1 was a **collaboration** with Adidas. It **dropped** with praise from both critics and fans. The collection's Boost sneakers sold out within 10 minutes.

Season 2 was released later that year at New York Fashion Week. *GQ Magazine* described it as "a little **dystopian**, a little future, and pretty wearable."

In 2016, Season 3 **debuted** at Madison Square Garden. It was followed by a listening party of West's album *The Life of Pablo*.

That same year, Adidas and Yeezy announced a long-term **collaboration**. Just one hour after the Boost 350 sneakers went on sale, they sold out everywhere.

In 2017, the Season 5 collection **dropped**, again spurring excitement from critics. The next year, West took out a full page ad in several newspapers announcing the Yeezy Boost Triple Whites.

In 2021, Yeezy and Gap signed a 10-year deal. Their **down** jacket was a fan favorite. The duo then **collaborated** with Balenciaga to release the second collection in 2022, helping bring a much younger customer base to Gap.

Yeezy has come a long way from a musician's vision to a fashion powerhouse. With West's creativity and knack for hype, the Yeezy brand will remain iconic for decades to come.

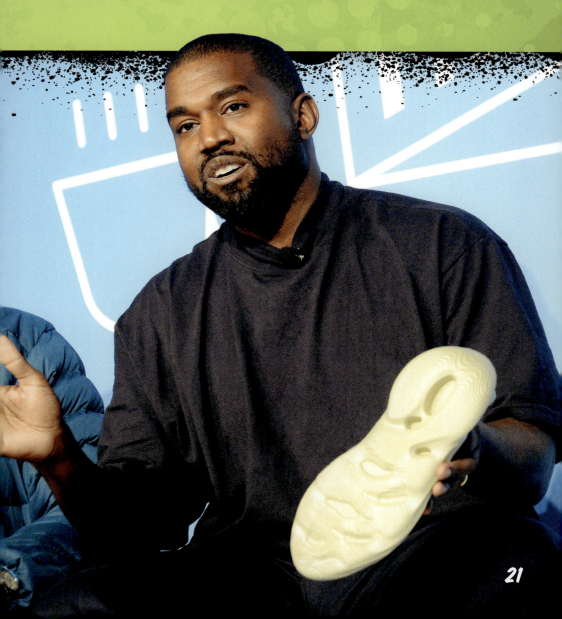

GLOSSARY

collaborate – to work with another person or group in order to do something or reach a goal.

debut – a first appearance.

down – the soft and warm under feathers from ducks or geese that can be used to insulate clothing items.

drop – when something that is highly anticipated is released to the public.

dystopia – an imagined society that is usually post-apocalyptic.

internship – when a student or graduate gains experience in a professional field.

platinum record – an award given to a musician whose album has sold one million copies or more.

prototype – an early sample, model, or release of a product created to test the idea.

ONLINE RESOURCES

To learn more about Yeezy, please visit **abdobooklinks.com** or scan this QR code. These links are routinely monitored and updated to provide the most current information available.

INDEX

Abloh, Virgil 12

Adidas (brand) 14, 17

Air Yeezy 10

Balenciaga (brand) 20

Boost sneakers 14, 17, 18

Fendi (brand) 12

Gap (brand) 20

GQ (magazine) 15

Grammy Awards 11

Jay-Z 6

Life of Pablo, The (album) 16

Madison Square Garden 16

New York Fashion Week 15

Nike (brand) 10

Off-White (brand) 12

Paris Fashion Week 12

West, Kanye 4, 6, 8, 11, 18, 21